GW00503329

ABOUT JOHN N. MERRILL

John combines the characteristics and strength of a mountain climber with the stamina and athletic capabilities of a marathon runner. In this respect he is unique and has to his credit a whole string of remarkable long walks. He is without question the world's leading marathon walker.

Over the last fifteen years he has walked more than 100,000 miles and successfully completed ten walks of at least 1,000 miles or more.

His six major walks in Great Britain are -
Hebridean Journey .... 1,003 miles
Northern Isles Journey .... 913 miles
Irish Island Journey .... 1,578 miles
Parkland Journey.. 2,043 miles
Lands End to John o'Groats .... 1,608 miles
and in 1978 he became the first person (permanent Guinness Book of Records entry) to walk the entire coastline of Britain — 6,824 miles in ten months.

In Europe he has walked across Austria — 712 miles — hiked the Tour of Mont Blanc, completed High Level Routes in the Dolomites and Italian Alps, and the GR20 route across Corsica in training! In 1982 he walked across Europe — 2,806 miles in 107 days — crossing seven countries, the Swiss and French Alps and the complete Pyrennean chain — the hardest and longest mountain walk in Europe, with more than 600,000 feet of ascent!

In America he used the world's longest footpath — The Appalachian Trail -2,200 miles — as a training walk. He has walked from Mexico to Canada via the Pacific Crest Trail in record time — 118 days for 2,700 miles. In Canada he has walked the Rideau Trail.

During the summer of 1984, John set off from Virginia Beach on the Atlantic coast, and walked 4,226 miles without a rest day, across the width of America to Santa Cruz and San Francisco on the Pacific Ocean. His walk is unquestionably his greatest achievement, being, in modern history, the longest, hardest crossing of the USA in the shortest time — under six months (178 days). The direct distance is 2,800 miles.

Between major walks John is out training in his own area — the Peak District National Park. As well as walking in other parts of Britain and Europe he has been trekking in the Himalayas five times. He has created more than ten challenge walks which have been used to raise more than £250,000 for charity. From his own walks he raised over £80,000. He is author of more than one hundred books, most of which he publishes himself. His book sales are in excess of 2½ million. He has created many long distance walks including The Limey Way and the Peakalnd Way. He lectures extensively in Britain and America.

CONTENTS

SHORT CIRCULAR WALKS

IN

SOUTH NOTTINGHAMSHIRE

BY

JOHN N. MERRILL

Maps and photographs by John N. Merrill.

a J.N.M.PUBLICATION

1989

a J.N.M. PUBLICATION

JNM PUBLICATIONS,
WINSTER,
MATLOCK,
DERBYSHIRE.
DE4 2DQ

Conceived, edited, typeset, designed, marketed and distributed by John N. Merrill.

© Text and routes — John N. Merrill 1989

© Maps and photographs — John N. Merrill 1989

First Published — July 1989

ISBN 0 907496 58 X

Printed by Netherwood Dalton & Co Ltd, Huddersfield

Set in Plantin — Roman and Bold.

Cover sketch — River Trent and Newark Castle by John Creber. © JNM Publications

INTRODUCTION

In 1985 I saw my book on walks in Nottinghamshire — Short Circular Walks in the Dukeries — published. I had long wanted to write this having spent fifteen years walking the area. With that one completed I began exploring the canals and soon realised what a mammoth task I had set myself. The first volume explored the Derbyshire and Nottinghamshire area — the Erewash, Beeston, Nottingham, and Chesterfield Canals. Unfortunately I had to stop upon reaching the Trent; there across it was the Grantham Canal, and what of the River Trent itself?

I therefore planned further books and at long last I began to explore southern Nottinghamshire and begin learning more about the River Trent, Grantham Canal, and Wolds area. For days I walked the area, continually being surprised at the beauty and history of the places I passed through. The task was most pleasurable with rights of way easy to find, well stiled and signed. Most of the footpaths have plastic yellow arrows on a white square and the bridleways a blue circle on a white square.

As always there were too many places to include but I have striven to give even coverage to all the types of walking to be found in the area. These include canal and river walks, woodland and hilly walks, and paths tracing history or exploring little known places. Despite many days walking, apart from a few people from nearby villages walking their dogs, I met no other walkers! Even on Easter Monday in a T shirt and shorts on the banks of the Trent no one was about!

As for my favourite walks, the West Leake Hills are a magnificent Wolds walk; the East Bridgford walk above the River Trent is outstanding; and the Lowdham walk links together some very interesting villages. This book continues where the Dukeries one left off and complements my Canal Walks Vol One — Derbyshire & Nottinghamshire — and Derby walks. Now I am looking at Leicestershire and the Charnwood Forest area which I first walked more than twenty years ago!

I have enjoyed immensely exploring and walking southern Nottinghamshire and hope these walks illustrate the tremendous walking there is in the area. Enjoy the walks and may I wish you HAPPY WALKING!

John N. Merrill.

JOHN N. MERRILL.
Derbyshire. 1989.

ABOUT THE WALKS -

Whilst every care is taken detailing and describing the walks in this book, it should be borne in mind that the countryside changes by the seasons and the work of man. I have described the walks to the best of my ability, detailing what I have found on the walk in the way of stiles and signs. Obviously with the passage of time stiles become broken or replaced by a ladder stile or even a small gate. Signs too have a habit of being broken or pushed over. All the routes follow rights of way and only on rare occasions will you have to overcome obstacles in its path, such as a barbed wire fence or electric fence.

The seasons bring occasional problems whilst out walking which should also be bourne in mind. In the height of summer paths become overgrown and you will have to fight your way through in a few places. In low lying areas the fields are often full of crops, and although the pathline goes straight across it may be more practical to walk round the field edge to get to the next stile or gate. In summer the ground is generally dry but in autumn and winter, especially because of our climate, the surface can be decidedly wet and slippery; sometimes even glutonous mud!

These comments are part of countryside walking which help to make your walk more interesting or briefly frustrating. Standing in a farmyard up to your ankles in mud might not be funny at the time but upon reflection was one of the highlights of the walk!

The mileage for each walk is based on three calculations — a. pedometer reading; b. the route map measured on the map; and c. the time I took for the walk. I believe the figure stated for each walk to be very accurate but we all walk differently and not always in a straight line! The time allowed for each walk is on the generous side and does not include pub stops. The figure is based on the fact that on average a person walks 2½ miles an hour but less in hilly terrain.

DOUBLE GATES ON RIVER TRENT PATH

2

SHELFORD LOCK

NEVILE ARMS, KINOULTON

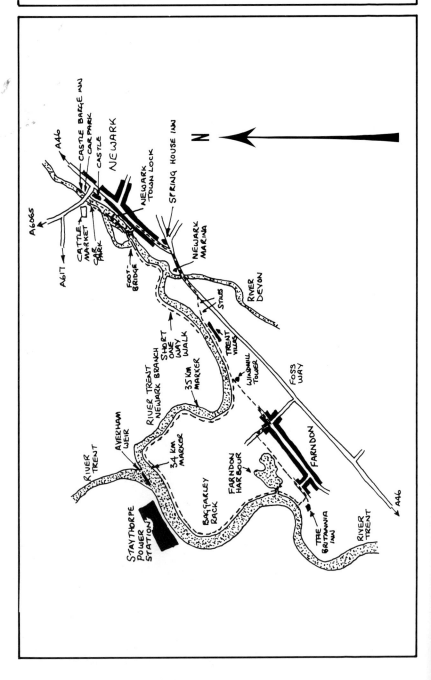

NEWARK ON TRENT — 6½ MILES

- allow 2½ hours.

MAP — O.S. 1:25,000 Pathfinder series — Sheet no 796 (SK 65/75) — Newark on Trent (West).

CAR PARK — Close to castle on either side of the River Trent.

INNS — Several close to the start in Newark, such as the Castle Bare Inn; and the Brittania Inn by the River Trent at Farndon close to the half way point of the walk.

BASIC ROUTE — Newark — Newark Town Lock — River Devon — Farndon — Farndon Harbour — River Trent — Baggarley Rack — Upper Water Mouth — River Trent (Newark Branch) — Newark Town Lock — Newark.

ABOUT THE WALK — Newark, its castle and River Trent is an imposing setting. The town itself is well worth exploring. The walk follows the River Trent along the opposite bank to the castle before crossing to the Town Lock and A46 road. ½ a mile of road walking brings you back to the river before crossing the lanes through Farndon to the harbour and river. Here you walk around a large penisula by the river seeing numerous wildfowl, rowers practising on the river, narrow boats passing by and other pleasure and commercial river traffic. You return to the A46 road and retrace your steps back to Newark and its castle.

A shorter one way return walk can be made along the northern bank of the River Trent from near the Town Lock. You cross a spectacular narrow stone bridge before gaining open fields and can walk along the bankside for a little over ½ a mile — about a 2½ mile return walk from the castle.

WALKING INSTRUCTIONS — From the car park near the Cattle Market gain the riverside and walk southwards away from the castle opposite and cross the footbridge over the river to the Town Lock. Keep the lock on your left and walk past the warehouses and dry docks to the road bridge just after the Trent Navigation Warehouse on your left. (Those on the shorter walk should keep straight ahead to the narrow stone bridge.) Turn left over the bridge and walk along Mill Lane to the main road. Turn right passing the Watermill Inn on your left and 200 yards later the Spring House Inn at the road junction. Keep to the righthand road passing Newark Marina and cross the bridge over the River Devon. About 100 yards later leave the road (A46) at the stile on the right of a gate. Cross the field to your left to a stile by the corrugated boundary wall. Walk beside it to another stile and narrow fenced path to a tarmaced road. Keep ahead to reach the banks of the River Trent and follow the path with Trent Villas on your left. There are several small gates along here. Continue past the houses along the bankside for a little over ¼ mile to the path sign on your right close to a windmill tower a little to your left. After doing the loop through Farndon and around the river you return to this point along the river bank.

Bear left at the path sign along the walled path past the windmill on your left. Keep ahead on a track at the junction just past the windmill and soon reach a road. Keep straight ahead on this past the houses for 200 yards to the cross roads close to house No 125 on Marsh Lane. Turn right along the track and in 100 yards turn left at the path sign following a track then path with Farndon Harbour on your right. You leave the harbour keeping straight ahead to a path sign and walk past a row of garages to the road. Continue straight ahead for a few yards to house No 9 and turn right down the signed path to the River Trent and picnic tables. To your left at Farndon Ferry is the Britannia Inn. Turn right and walk along the banks of the River Trent for the next two miles to where you left it earlier close to the windmill tower. En route you look across at Staythorpe Power Station and Upper Water Mouth. Retrace your steps back to Trent Villas, the A46 road, Mill Lane, and Town Lock back to the car park and Newark Castle.

NEWARK — is steeped in Civil War history with many fortifications remaining. The ruined castle was started in 1173 but much of the river facade dates from the 14th and 15th centuries. The castle was a Royalist stronghold and held out three times against the roundheads. In 1646 it was finally taken by the roundheads and they dismantled the castle. A walk around the town is of particular note. The 15th century White Hart Inn in the Market is the oldest building. Others of particular note are the half timbered Governors House where several Governor's resided during the Civil War. The parish church dedicated to St. Mary Magdalene is a prominent landmark. The local museum in Appletree Gate has many exhibits from the Civil War. The Castle Barge on the river is an unusual inn, being a former grain barge.

CASTLE BARGE INN, NEWARK

NEWARK LOCK AND CASTLE

RIVER TRENT NAVIGATION, NEWARK

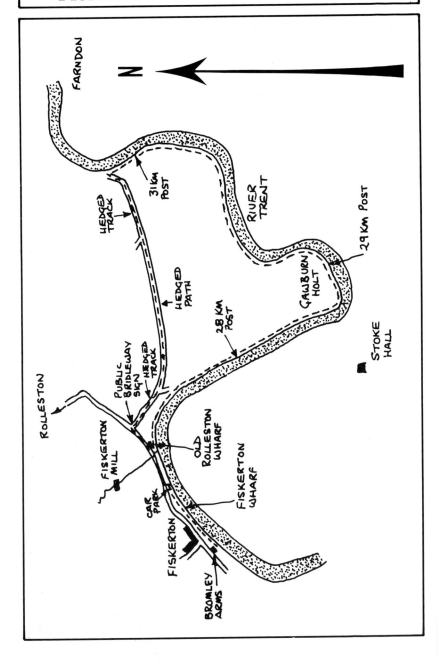

FISKERTON (NORTH) — 4½ MILES

- allow 2 hours.

MAP — O.S. 1:25,000 Pathfinder series Sheer No. 796 (SK 65/75) — Newark on Trent (West).

CAR PARK — eastern side of Fiskerton.

INN — Bromley Arms, Fiskerton.

BASIC ROUTE — Fiskerton — River Trent — Gawburn Holt — River Trent — Bridleway — Fiskerton.

ABOUT THE WALK — A beautiful, remote and unspoilt section of river walking. Numerous wildfowl — swans, Canada geese, mallards and others are frequently seen. Across the river is the impressive Stoke Hall. You start at Fiskerton, one of the gems of the river, and follow the bank side for more than half the walk. You return along a bridleway back to Fiskerton and its impressive wharf.

WALKING INSTRUCTIONS — From the car park walk along the road away from Fiskerton to the stream from Fiskerton Mill. Here where the road turns gently left go through the gate on your right and past the house on your left- Old Rolleston Wharf. The path here is beautifully maintained and just beyond the house are seats. For the next two miles you keep to the river banks; sometimes on a faint path and others along the top of dikes. There are several double white gates, a feature of the River Trent, to pass through. Pass kilometer markers 29, 30 and 31. Just past the latter you cross two small footbridges with a marshy area on your left. Just after is a gate and here you leave the river and begin following a bridleway. At first it is a hedged track and in a ⅓ mile where it turns right you keep straight ahead on a hedged path. Little over ½ mile later it becomes a track again and you follow this to the Rolleston/Fiskerton road. Turn left and you are soon back to the riverside as you retrace your steps back to the car park and Fiskerton Wharf.

FISKERTON WHARF

9

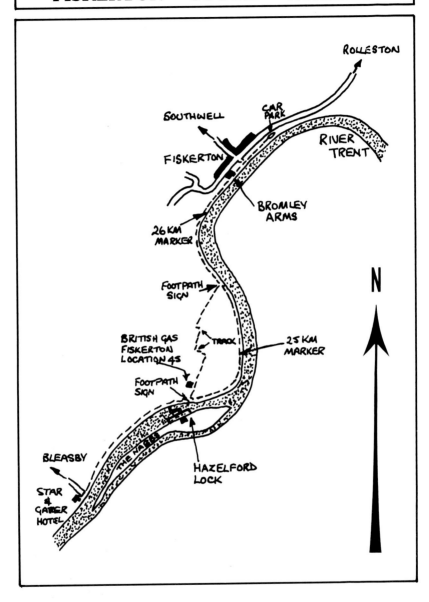

FISKERTON (SOUTH) — 3½ AND 4½ MILES.

- allow 1½ to 2 hours.

MAPS — O.S. 1:25,000 Pathfinder series sheets Nos 796 (SK 65/75) — Newark on Trent. Sheet No 813 (SK 64/74) — Carlton and Elston.

CAR PARK — East side of Fiskerton Wharf.

INNS — Bromley Arms, Fiskerton. Star and Garter Hotel, Hazelford Ferry.

BASIC ROUTE — Fiskerton — River Trent — Hazelford Lock — Hazelford Ferry — reurn the same way or along path from lock to near Fiskerton.

ABOUT THE WALK- A beautiful section of river with the Trent Hills in the background. En route you pass Hazelford Lock and its impressive right-angled weir. Here you can return along another path to Fiskerton or continue ahead to the Star and Garter Hotel at Hazelford Ferry. You return the same way.

WALKING INSTRUCTIONS — From the car park on the eastern side of Fiskerton walk along the tarmaced path beside the houses of Fiskerton and the Bromley Arms Inn. Continue along the bankside passing Kilometer markers 26 and 25. En route notice the path sign on your right; this is where the path from Hazelford Lock regains the bankside. Keep along the path to Hazelford Lock. Just before it is the path sign on your right. For those on the longer walk continue by the river for ½ mile to the Star and Garter Hotel at Hazelford Ferry; you return the same way back to Fiskerton. For those on the shorter walk, from the lock take the signed path by the field edge for a few yards before turning right, as signed, and crossing the field to the British Gas Fiskerton Location 45. Keep the field boundary on your left then cross an open section to the field boundary on your left again. 50 yards later reach a track on your left. Turn left along this and follow it to your right. Then left and immediately turn right onto another. At the end continue ahead with the field boundary on your right to the bankside and path sign you saw earlier. Turn left and follow the path back to Fiskerton, passing through the double white gates.

STOKE LOCK AND WEIR

11

HOVERINGHAM — 5½ MILES

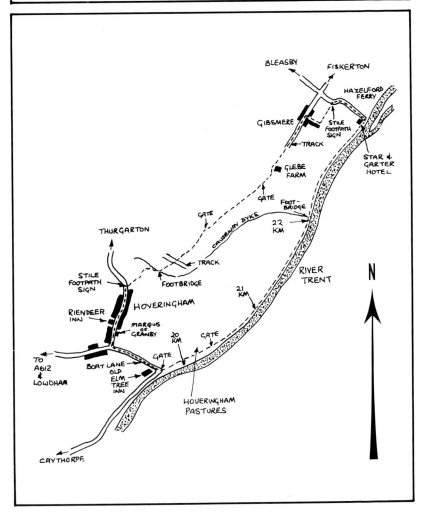

COMMERCIAL BARGE ON RIVER TRENT NR HOVERINGHAM

HOVERINGHAM — 5½ MILES

- allow 2¼ hours.

MAP — O.S. 1:25,000 Pathfinder series — Sheet No 813 — SK 64/74 — Carlton and Elston.

CAR PARK — No official one. Off road parking on Hoveringham Road, south of Elm Tree Inn.

INNS — Elm Tree Inn, Hoveringham; Star & Garter Hotel, Hazelford Ferry; Reindeer Inn and Marquis of Granby in Hoveringham village.

BASIC ROUTE — Elm Tree Inn, Hoveringham — River Trent — Star & Garter Hotel, Hazelford Ferry — Gibsmere — Glebe Farm — Hoveringham — Elm Tree Inn.

ABOUT THE WALK — A delightful stretch of river with the eastern side high wooded slopes of the Trent Hills. Gliders can be seen taking to the air on the right and to the left windsurfers cross a large lagoon. Swans, Canada Geese, ducks, and grey herons are frequently seen, while on the river pleasure craft and river barges pass by. You return along a bridleway to the attractive Hoveringham village before following Boat Lane back to the river Trent.

WALKING INSTRUCTIONS — Walk along Hoveringham Road to the Elm Tree Inn on the lefthand corner. Leave the road at the gate and follow the path close to the river; heading northwards for the next 2 miles to the Star and Garter Hotel at Hazelford Ferry, en route passing kilometer signs — 20 to 22. At the Star and Garter Hotel leave the river and follow the road towards Bleasby for ¼ mile. Follow it round a lefthand bend and where it starts a righthand bend is the stile and footpath sign on your left. Keep the field boundary on your right and walk to the Manor House, gate and path sign. Turn right down the lane into Gibsmere. At the village road turn left and walk past Little Glebe Farm onto a track and signed bridleway. The pathline is well signed with blue arrows indicating a bridleway. Continue to Glebe Farm. Just after keep to the left to a gate and track. Continue ahead on a grass track keeping the field boundary on your right then hedge on your left and in ¾ mile cross a footbridge and track. Continue straight ahead on a grass track to a footbridge. Cross this and walk around the field to your right before crossing a field to a stile and path sign on the edge of Hoveringham village. Turn left through the village past the Reindeer Inn and Marquis of Granby to the road junction. Turn left along Boat Lane back to the River Trent and Elm Tree Inn.

HOVERINGHAM — From near the Elm Tree Inn a ferry operated across the Trent to Kneeton which lies high above the wooded slopes.

EAST BRIDGFORD — 5 MILES

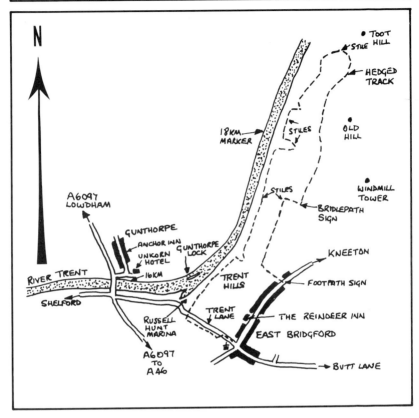

GUNTHORPE LOCK AND RIVER TRENT FROM TRENT HILLS

EAST BRIDGFORD — 5 MILES

- allow 2 hours

MAP — O.S. 1:25,000 Pathfinder Series Sheet No. 813 — SK 64/74 — Carlton and Elston.

CAR PARK — No official one. The walk starts from the Main Street in East Bridgford.

INN — The Reindeer Inn, East Bridgford.

BASIC ROUTE — East Bridgford — Trent Hills — Watson's Piece — Old Hill — East Bridgford.

ABOUT THE WALK — An absolutely stunning walk high above the River Trent with matchless views of the river and Gunthorpe Lock. You walk high above the river by woodland for 2 miles. You return to East Bridgford along a bridleway with extensive views before walking through the unspoilt village. One of the finest river walks in Nottinghamshire!

WALKING INSTRUCTIONS — Starting from the main street in East Bridgford, near the Reindeer Inn, walk along the street to the cross roads below the church. Turn right down Trent Lane and just past the high church walls on your left, turn left at the path sign and follow this path beside the field edge and above the lane for ¼ mile before descending to the lane. Cross and ascend the driveway on the signposted footpath. Reach a stile at the top and begin following the well defined stiled path along the Trent Hills, keeping to the lefthand edge of the field with woodland on your left. The views are superb down to the river and Gunthorpe Lock. There is a path along the bank of the river but it cannot equal this high level path. Keep to this path for the next two miles. On the way you will walk inland four times to walk around shallow valleys. Yellow arrow signs and stiles guide you. After the fourth one you move away from the river and shortly afterwards reach a stile and descend "Watson's Piece" to a small pond. Here bear right on a level track and reach the end of a hedged track — a bridlepath.

You now follow this ascending track over the slopes of Old Hill for a mile to a T junction of tracks by a bridlepath sign. Turn right down the track for 50 yards to a stile on your left. Turn left and keep the field hedge on your left — it is a grass slope at first. After ¼ mile continue ahead across an open field to its middle and turn left on a path to the road, gained at a footpath sign, on the northern outskirts of East Bridgford. Turn right and walk through the village to the Reindeer Inn.

EAST BRIDGFORD — Trent Lane once had a toll bridge across the river, but this has long since gone with the building of the bridge at Gunthorpe — the only bridge across the river between Newark and Nottingham.

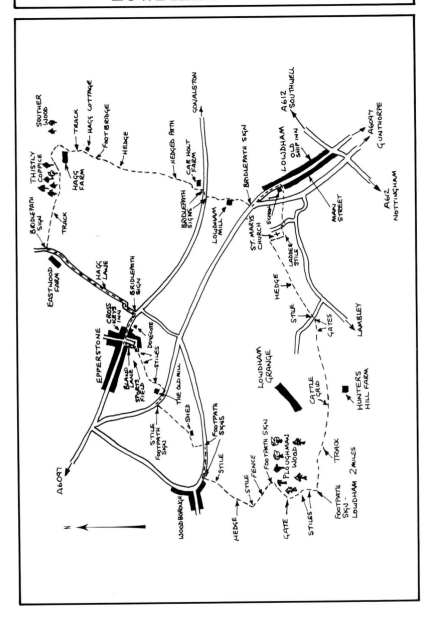

LOWDHAM — 8 MILES

- allow 3½ hours.

MAP — O.S. 1:25,000 Pathfinder Series Sheet No 813 — SK 64/74 — Carlton and Elston.

CAR PARK — No official one.

INNS — The Old Ship Inn, Lowdham and Cross Keys, Epperstone.

BASIC ROUTE — Lowdham — Lowdham Mill — Hagg Farm — Eastwood Farm — Hagg Lane — Epperstone — Woodborough — Ploughman Wood — Hunters Hill — St Mary's Church — Lowdham.

ABOUT THE WALK — Starting from Lowdham you walk past the beautifully attractive Lowdham Mill before ascending on a good path/track to Hagg Cottage and Farm. You descend Hagg Lane to gain Epperstone and its dovecotes. You cross further fields past another former mill before skirting Woodborough and ascending to the edge of Ploughman's Wood. The remainder of the walk is down hill beneath Lowdham Grange to St. Mary's Church and into Lowdham. Although one of the longest walks in the book, it is a really pleasant one full of interest and through gentle rolling countryside.

WALKING INSTRUCTIONS — Starting from the northern end of the Main Street in Lowdham, walk past the Church of England School on your left and continue up the road to the junction with the dual-laned A6097 road. Turn sharp right just before the road onto the drive to Lowdham Mill; bridlepath signed. Follow the drive towards the house but close to its entrance gates bear right as signed and walk past the mill on its righthand side. Continue ahead with the mill leat on your left for a short distance before bearing slightly right and walking up the field edge to Gonalston Lane and a bridlepath sign. Turn right then left at another bridlepath sign just before Car Holt Farm. The bridlepath is well defined and for the next ½ mile is a hedged path. Afterwards continue ahead with the hedge on your right and soon cross a footbridge and keep to the lefthand side of Hagg Cottage. Just past it join a track which you follow towards Hagg Farm. Keep to the right of the buildings on a track and shortly past the buildings turn left on a track — this is the right of way and not the one shown on the Ordnance Survey map. Follow the track to the edge of Thistly Coppice and turn left on a track keeping the wood on your right for the next ¼ mile. The route is well signed with blue arrows — a bridleway. Leaving the wood you keep ahead on the track which keeps close to the hedge on your right then left. Gain the tarmaced lane — Hagg Lane — to the right of Eastwood Farm. Turn left and descend the lane to Epperstone.

At the road in Epperstone turn right through the village, passing a solitary Dovecote in a field on your left. A little further is the Cross Keys Inn and Post Office and store on your right. Just afterwards take the second road on your left — Bland Lane. At the end turn right past the houses to a path sign and stile. Cross the fields guided by stiles keeping to the left of the edge of the sports field. Gain more stiles and footbridges and walk around the lefthand side of a former mill to the A6097 road. Turn right and in a few yards left at the footpath sign and stile. The path is defined across a field to the next where the hedge is on your left. At the end of the next field the path is on the immediate right of a large shed. Follow it to the end of the field and turn left to the road — Lowdham Lane — by a pathsign. Turn right towards Woodborough village.

After nearly ¼ mile on the outskirts of the village turn left, as footpath signed — Lowdham 3 miles. You keep to the righthand side of the field to a stile and then walk along the tarmaced drive to a caravan site. At its entrance go through the small metal gate on your left and continue on the well defined path along the field edge to another stile. On reaching the next field turn left and ascend the field edge to Ploughman Wood. At the top turn right beside the wood and walk along the field edge to a gate at the wood's end. Turn left through this and continue with the wood on your left and cross two stiles leaving the wood behind and in less than ¼ mile reach another path sign — Lowdham 2 miles. Turn left on the defined path which after the first field becomes track and descend for ½ mile to the sharp righthand bend in the road for Hunters Hill Farm. Keep straight ahead keeping the hedge/fence on your left for a ⅓ mile to a gate. Turn left over a footbridge and cross the narrow field to the road to Lowdham Grange. Cross over to a stile and continue with the hedge on your left. You are aiming for St. Mary's Church and its spire acts as a useful guide. Keep the field boundary on your left and walk around the field to the right of the church to a ladder stile. Over this walk through the churchyard to a track. Turn right then left on a signed path — Lowdham village. Keep the stream on your left and in the righthand field can be seen the outline of a motte. Cross the A6097 road and continue on the path to the right of the Church of England School. Turn right along Main Street back into central Lowdham.

LOWDHAM — Much of St. Mary's Church dates from the 15th century. Lowdham Grange was built in the 1930's as a borstal.

EPPERSTONE — has two dovecotes and the church dates from Norman times.

LOWDHAM MILL

DOVECOTE, EPPERSTONE

FOOTPATH NOTICE NEAR WOODBOROUGH MILL

ST. MARY'S CHURCH, LOWDHAM

19

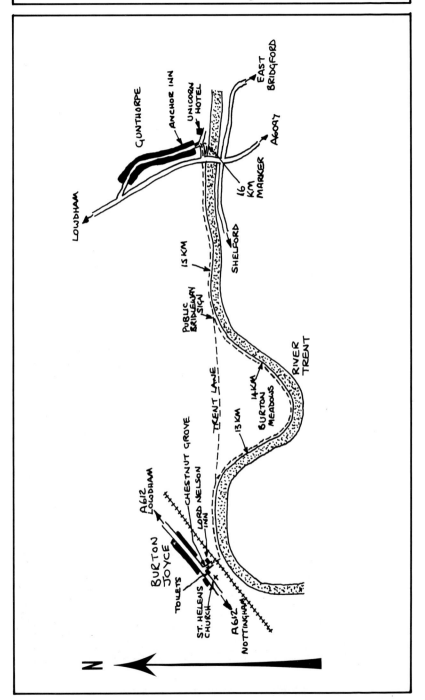

GUNTHORPE AND BURTON JOYCE — 5 MILES

- allow 2 hours.

MAP — O.S. 1:25,000 Pathfinder Series Sheet No. 813 — SK 64/74 — Carlton and Elston.

CAR PARK — No official one at Gunthorpe or Burton Joyce; but road side parking at either place.

INNS — Anchor Inn and Unicorn Hotel at Gunthorpe. Lord Nelson Inn, Burton Joyce.

BASIC ROUTE — Gunthorpe — River Trent — Trent Lane — River Trent — Burton Joyce — River Trent — Burton Meadows — Gunthorpe.

ABOUT THE WALK — A beautiful stretch of the River Trent between Gunthorpe and Burton Joyce. The walk can be started from either end but the walking instructions commence from Gunthorpe. If starting from Burton Joyce, start from Chestnut Grove near the church and pass the Lord Nelson Inn and cross the railway line to gain the river; here turn left for Trent Lane and Burton Meadows.

WALKING INSTRUCTIONS — From Gunthorpe and the Unicorn Hotel gain the river path near the 16km marker. Turn right and walk under the road bridge and continue along the riverside (the river on your left) for the next mile. A ¼ mile after the 15km marker, where the river curves left keep straight ahead on the bridlepath on a hedged track. You keep on this for ¾ mile to the river again. Burton Joyce is ½ mile further along the river, where you turn right to cross the railway line and into Chestnut Grove. If not going there turn left and now walk with the river on your right around Burton Meadows passing the 13km and 14km markers. You soon rejoin your starting out path and retrace your steps back to Gunthorpe.

UNICORN HOTEL, GUNTHORPE

21

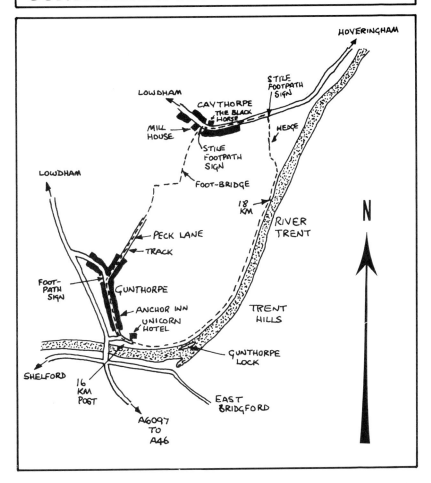

THE RIVER TRENT — is navigable from Shardlow to Gainsborough and the Humber River and links several canals together — the Trent & Mersey; Erewash Canal; Beeston and Nottingham Canal; Fossdyke Navigation and the Chesterfield Canal. The river has been a trading route for centuries and two Bronze Age canoes found near Nottingham confirm the importance of the river from at least 1000 B.C. Although the river had navigation protection for centuries it was not until 1783 that the Trent Navigation Company was formed. They began improving the waterway and building locks. The river was popular in the 19th Century when the adjoining canals were at their highest but like them the railways brought about their decline. Today, as with the canals, maintenance and care of the waterway is looked after by the British Waterways Board.

GUNTHORPE — A ferry once operated here across the river to link with East Bridgford. In 1875 a toll bridge was built. This has now gone and the road bridge built early this century forms the only road crossing of the river between Newark and Nottingham.

GUNTHORPE AND CAYTHORPE — 4½ MILES

- allow 1¾ hours.

MAP — O.S. 1:25,000 Pathfinder Series Sheet No 813 — SK 64/74 — Carlton and Elston.

CAR PARK — No official one.

INNS — Unicorn Hotel and Anchor Inn, Gunthorpe; The Black Horse, Caythorpe.

BASIC ROUTE — Gunthorpe — Gunthorpe Lock — River Trent — Hoveringham Road — Caythorpe — Peck Lane — Gunthorpe.

ABOUT THE WALK — Starting from Gunthorpe and its attractive setting you walk first to Gunthorpe Lock, no doubt seeing water skiing in the area, before continuing on beside the river Trent for 1½ miles. You cross fields to the picturesque village of Caythorpe and opposite the inn and old mill cross further fields back to Gunthorpe.

WALKING INSTRUCTIONS — Gain the river bank footpath near the Unicorn Hotel and walk northwards along it first to Gunthorpe Lock and on beside the river for a further 1½ miles. Across the river are the wooded cliffs of the Trent Hills, walked on the East Bridgford walk. Less than ¼ mile after passing the 18km marker post and just after crossing a small stream — Car Dyke — leave the riverside and bear diagonally left across the field to the top lefthand corner. Bear left then right keeping the hedge on your right as you walk along the field edge to a stile, path sign and Hoveringham Road. Turn left along the road into Caythorpe village. Just after the Black Horse Inn on your right, turn left at the stile with yellow path arrow and walk past Mill House. Keep the field boundary on your right and gain a footbridge. Continue with the field boundary on your left to another footbridge. Cross another soon afterwards and turn right and before the end of the field turn left and in 250 yards reach the end of Peck Lane. Follow this track for almost ½ mile to Gunthorpe village. Turn left along the main street past the Anchor Inn and back to the Unicorn Hotel, river and 16km marker post.

TRENT BRIDGE, GUNTHORPE

23

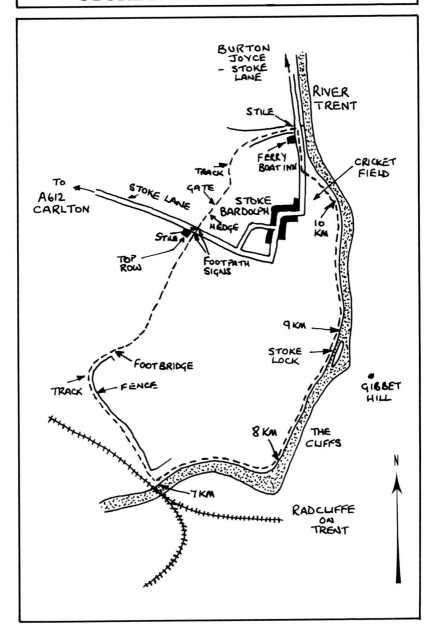

STOKE BARDOLPH — 5 MILES

- allow 2 hours.

MAPS — O.S. 1:25,000 Pathfinder Series Sheets Nos 813 — SK 64/74 — Carlton and Elston; and Sheet No 834 — SK 63/73 — Radcliffe on Trent & Keyworth.

CAR PARK — Beside the River Trent at Stoke Bardolph; near the Ferry Boat Inn.

INN — The Ferry Boat Inn, Stoke Bardolph.

BASIC ROUTE — Stoke Bardolph — River Trent — Stoke Lock — River Trent — Ouse Dyke — Stoke Lane — Ferry Boat Inn.

ABOUT THE WALK — A stunning section of the river Trent with impressive cliffs on the Radcliffe on Trent side. Half way along the river you walk past Stoke Lock set in woodland — a delightful location. Where the railway crosses the river you walk inland on a track before crossing the fields to Stoke Lane and onto the river Trent at the Ferry Boat Inn, Stoke Bardolph.

WALKING INSTRUCTIONS — From near the Ferry Boat Inn on Stoke Lane, Stoke Bardolph, walk along the road to where it leaves the riverside and bear left on a track, at first a little way from the river. On your right is the cricket field. Pass the 10km marker and soon afterwards you keep close to the river to the 9km marker and Stoke Lock. Walk past the lock and continue on the bankside for just over a mile to the 7km marker and railbridge over the River Trent.

Turn right before the bridge onto a track; keep the railway above you on your left and the earth walls of lagoons on your right. After ½ mile and at the end of the lagoons turn right onto another track keeping the fence on your right. In 200 yards reach a footbridge over the Ouse Dyke. Cross it and turn right then left. You cross two fields on an ill-defined path. Basically you aim for the right of a group of houses known as Top Row. After the second field you walk beside a hedge on your left close to the houses and gain Stoke Lane at a gate beside a path sign. Cross the lane to a stile and path sign and follow the path by the hedge on your right to a gate. Continue ahead with the hedge on your right to a track. Bear left along this for 50 yards and after crossing a small dyke turn right and walk beside it then inbetween two dykes to reach Stoke Lane close to Ferry Boat Inn, reached via a stile.

FERRY BOAT INN — STOKE BARDOLPH

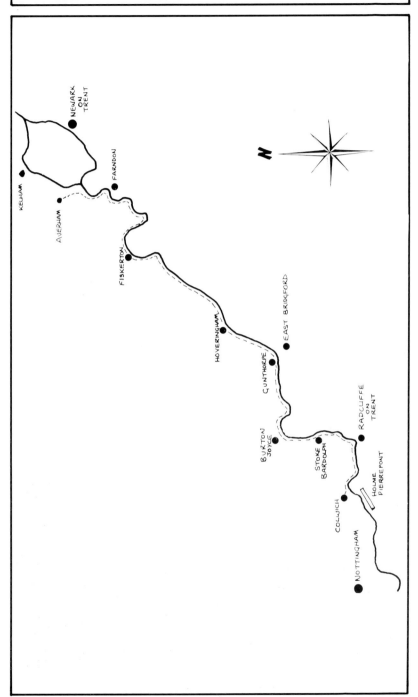

FISKERTON to COLWICK — via the River Trent — 15 MILES

- allow 5 to 6 hours.

MAPS — O.S. 1:50,000 Landranger Series — Sheet No 120 — Mansfield, Worksop & surrounding area. Sheet No. 129 — Nottingham & Loughborough area.

INNS — at Fiskerton, Hazelford Ferry, Hoveringham, Gunthorpe, and Stoke Bardolph.

BASIC ROUTE — The River Trent from Fiskerton to Colwich, Nottingham.

ABOUT THE WALK — Unlike the other walks in this book this is an end to end walk and a culmination of all the walks along the River Trent. All of them basically interlock, and by using the River Trent portions of the maps and text you can walk end to end. It would make a very pleasant weekend walk stopping overnight at a local inn or as a bit of challenge to walk 15 miles in a day! At the Colwich end of the walk, walk under the railway bridge near Radcliffe on Trent close to the 7km marker post. Continue by the river for a little over ½ mile to where the first road reaches the Trent on your right. Turn right along this then left to central Colwich. The walk can be extended by 3 miles in the north by starting at Averham, near the church. You gain the river near Staythorpe Power Station.

RIVER TRENT — BURTON MEADOWS

27

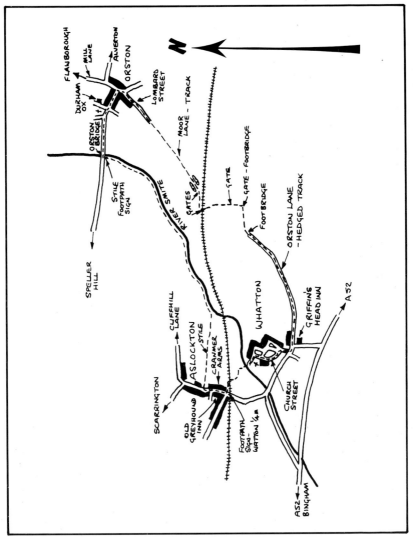

WHATTON — The church dates from the 14th century. In the north aisle is a monument to Robert de Whatton, a vicar here in 1304. An alabaster floor tomb has an engraved portrait to Thomas Cranmer dated 1501. He was born in Aslockton and went on to become Archbishop of Canterbury.

ASLOCKTON — As one of the inns records — Cranmer Arms — it was the birthplace of Thomas Cranmer, the Archbishop of Canterbury. The Motte and Bailey was in former days referred to as Cranmer's Mound for he often played here during the first 14 years of his life here. He went on to lead a prominent life in London and married King Henry the Eighth to Anne Boleyn. He played a major role in the Reformation and dissolution of monasteries.

WHATTON AND ORSTON — 5½ MILES

- allow 2¼ hours.

MAPS — O.S. 1:25,000 Pathfinder Series Sheet No. 813 — SK 64/74 — Carlton and Elston, and Sheet No. 834 — SK 63/73 — Radcliffe on Trent & Keyworth.

CAR PARK — No official one.

INNS — Griffin's Head Inn, Whatton; Durham Ox, Orston; and Cranmer Arms and Old Greyhound Inn, Aslockton.

BASIC ROUTE — Whatton — Orston Lane — Moor Lane — Orston — Orston Bridge — River Smite — Aslockton — Whatton.

ABOUT THE WALK — From Whatton you follow old lanes to the picturesque village of Orston; winner of the best kept village (population 300-700) in Nottinghamshire. From here you walk beside the River Smite to Aslockton. A short walk from here returns you to Whatton.

WALKING INSTRUCTIONS — Starting from the Griffin's Head Inn in Whatton, walk down the lefthand lane — Orston Lane. After leaving the houses this becomes a hedged track. After ¾ mile at the end of the track cross a footbridge and turn right walking around the field to a gate and footbridge. Turn sharp left keeping the field boundary on your left and in ¼ mile cross a railway line and turn right to a gate. Through this you are on another track — Moor Lane — which first passes between two small lakes. In ½ mile reach the outskirts of Orston and continue ahead now on a tarmaced road — Lombard Street. At the main road turn left (Mill Lane) and left almost immediately onto Longbrou road. On your right is the plaque recording the winners of the best kept village competition.

Continue along the road past the Post Office and Durham Ox Inn, keeping straight ahead at all road junctions. The last house on your right is particularly fine. You are now on Smite Lane and in ¼ mile reach Orston Bridge over the River Smite. On the other side of the bridge turn left at the footpath sign and stile. The path line is not what is shown on the Ordnance Survey map going through the centre of the fields towards Aslockton. Instead you keep close to the bankside of the River Smite for the next 1½ miles. The pathline is defined and well stiled. Just before you near the railway bridge over the river turn right, as footpath signed, and walk along the field edge with the boundary on your left. At the end of the second field cross a stile by a footpath sign and walk past Saucer Farm with the remains of a Motte and Bailey in the field on your right. You walk along the farm track to reach the road in Aslockton via a gate beside a pathsign. Turn left through the village passing the Cranmer Arms Inn and Old Greyhound Inn; the latter states — "Good Stabling". Just after turn left at the footpath sign — Whatton ¼ mile. The path is tarmaced and leads around the fields and over the river Smite to Whatton church. Turn right at the road junction — Church Street — and follow the road down to the main road. Turn left and in a few yards is the Griffin's Head Inn.

ORSTON — Much of the church is 13th century but the tower is 18th century in classical style.

29

HOUSE AT ORSTON

ORSTON CHURCH

BEST KEPT VILLAGE PLAQUE, ORSTON

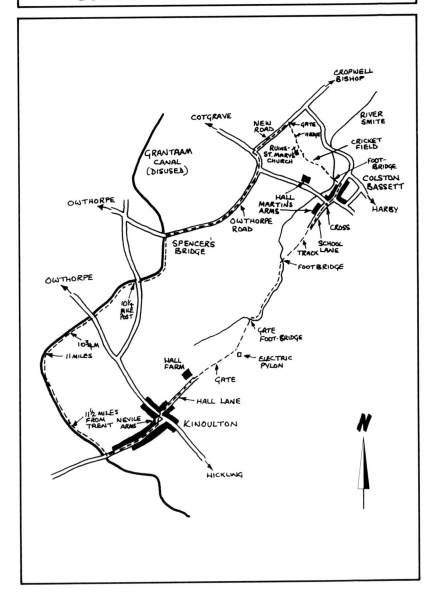

COLSTON BASSETT — The 15ft high Cross is National Trust property and was rebuilt last century on an old base. The present spired church was built in 1892. The ruined St. Mary's Church dates from the 13th Century but has Norman remains. The bells and font were taken to the new church. The Bassett family who founded the impressive Hall gave their name to the village.

COLSTON BASSETT AND THE GRANTHAM CANAL — 7 MILES

- allow 3 hours.

MAP — O.S. 1:25,000 Pathfinder Series Sheet No. 834 — SK 63/73 — Radcliffe on Trent & Keyworth.

CAR PARK — No official one.

INNS — Martin's Arms, Colston Bassett; Nevile Arms, Kinoulton.

BASIC ROUTE — Colston Bassett — River Smite — Hall Farm — Kinoulton — Grantham Canal — Spencer's Bridge — Owthorpe Road — St. Mary's Church — Colston Bassett.

ABOUT THE WALK — A stunning walk full of history and attractive scenery. Longer than most in this book but easily worth the extra miles! Volume Five of my Canal Walk series details many walks on the Grantham Canal. Starting from Colston Bassett and its historic Cross you cross fields on a bridlepath to Kinoulton. Here you reach the disused Grantham Canal and follow it for nearly two miles to Spencer's Bridge. A short road walk brings you near Colston Bassett and in the final mile you pass the derelict St. Mary's Church.

WALKING INSTRUCTIONS — Starting from the Cross in Colston Bassett walk along School Lane and pass Martin's Inn on your right. At the start of the lane is a footpath sign — Kinoulton & Hickling. Follow the lane to its end at a gate and bridlepath sign. Continue ahead on a track with the hedge on your left and in just over ¼ mile pass through a gate and cross the infant River Smite via a footbridge. Keep the river on your left for the next ⅓ mile to another gate and footbridge. Cross the river and ascend the field slightly leftwards to the right of an electric pylon. Bear right and aim for the lefthand side of Hall Farm ¼ mile ahead. You gain Hall lane via a gate beside a bridlepath sign. Follow the lane into Kinoulton village, bearing left to cross the green in front of the Nevile Arms. Continue ahead on the road through the village passing Pinfold Lane, the Old Bakehouse and St. Lukes Church. Just after reach the Grantham Canal and turn right onto the towpath — don't cross the bridge.

Follow the towpath with the canal on your left for the next 1¾ miles. On the way pass several mile markers — 11½ miles from the Trent — and eventually — 10¼ miles from the Trent. From this marker continue beside the canal for a further ¼ mile to the Owthorpe Road at Spencer's Bridge. Here leave the canal and turn right along the road and keep on it for the next ¾ mile. At the road junction turn left and a few yards later turn right on New Road, signposted for Cropwell Bishop. Keep on this for less than ¼ mile to a gate on your right. Turn right keeping the hedge on your left to reach the ruins of St. Mary's church. Walk past the ruins on your right and descend to a gate. Bear slightly left aiming for the immediate right of the cricket pavilion. Continue across parkland to a footbridge over the River Smite and ascend to the road in Colston Bassett. Turn right, passing the church on your left back to the Cross and road junction where you began.

GRANTHAM CANAL AND PLAQUE AT KINOULTON

GRANTHAM CANAL — In November 1791 the capital — £40,000 — was raised at a single meeting for the construction of the canal from the River Trent at Nottingham to Grantham. The canal was a useful waterway last century but like so many suffered badly from rail competition. In 1905 18,802 tons were carried and by 1924 this had dwindled to 1,583 tons. Five years later in 1929 it was closed. Today it is sadly derelict with many of the bridges now gone; sections without water and badly overgrown; and other sections particularly attractive and well preserved as this walk shows. The Grantham Canal Restoration Society have placed informative plaques where a road crosses the canal.

GRANTHAM CANAL NR KINOULTON

COLSTON BASSETT CROSS

CLIPSTON — 4 MILES

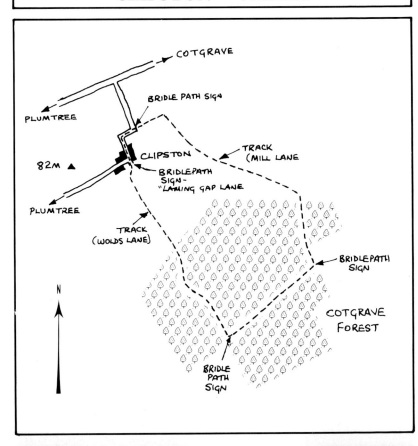

COTGRAVE FOREST

CLIPSTON AND COTGRAVE FOREST — 4 MILES

- allow 1½ hours.

MAP — O.S. 1:25,000 Pathfinder Series Sheet No. 834 — SK 63/73 — Radcliffe on Trent & Keyworth.

CAR PARK — No official one.

INN — None on the walk, nearest at Cotgrave a mile away.

BASIC ROUTE — Clipston — Wolds Lane — Cotgrave Forest — Mill Lane — Clipston.

ABOUT THE WALK — A short walk in forest well to the south of the wellknown Sherwood Forest. The whole walk is on tracks in the forest which in the wetter months can be quite boggy. The views in the latter half are extensive to Nottingham and its airport. A variety of birds, flowers and butterflies can be seen.

WALKING INSTRUCTIONS — From the rightangled bend in the road in the centre of the hamlet of Clipston keep straight ahead on a track signposted — Bridlepath — Laming Gap Lane. The track descends a little before ascending gently to Cotgrave Forest. Just after entering the forest the track loops to your right and ¼ mile later just before crossing a small stream the track becomes straight. ¼ mile later and close to the forest edge on your right turn left onto a another track, as bridlepath signed. You keep on this track for ⅔ mile to its eastern edge. Here where signed — bridleway — turn left on the track, first beside the wood then through it and in less ½ mile reach a crossroads of bridlepaths at a corner of forest on your right. Turn left and follow another track, known as Mill Lane, and follow this for a mile back to Clipston. The track turns sharp left in the final stages and reaches the minor road just north of Clipston by a bridlepath sign. Turn left and follow the road back to Clipston where you began.

GRANTHAM CANAL MILE POST

37

BUNNY — 6 MILES

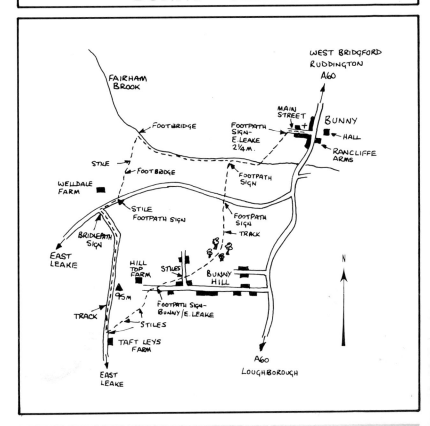

FAIRHAM BROOK NEAR BUNNY

BUNNY — The Parkyns family have played an important role in the village and area for centuries. One member of the family, Lord Rancliffe, planted Rancliffe Wood and the trees on Windmill Hill. The hall was built by the family and has an impressive tower with a large coat of arms upon it. Near the church are four almshouses also built by the Parkyns with latin inscriptions. The church dates from the 14th century and has many monuments to the Parkyns. The most famous was Thomas Parkyns who became known as the Wrestling Baronet in the 18th century. His lifesize monument shows him ready for a bout.

BUNNY AND BUNNY HILL — 6 MILES

- allow 2½ hours.

MAPS — O.S. 1:25,000 Pathfinder Series Sheet No SK42/52.
- O.S. 1:50,000 Landranger Series Sheet No 129 — Nottingham & Lough-borough area.

CAR PARK — no official one.

INN — Rancliffe Arms, Bunny.

BASIC ROUTE — Bunny — Bunny Hill — Taft Leys Farm — Trig 95 metres — Welldale Farm — Fairham Brook — Bunny.

ABOUT THE WALK — Bunny, although now on a major road — A60 — has several fine buildings worth exploring. The walk takes you across fields to the summit of Bunny Hill and its vantage point. You descend the other side to a hedged track and cross the hills back towards Bunny. You follow the Fairham Brook back to the village. A pleasant walk with distant views on little used paths; all are well stiled and signed.

WALKING INSTRUCTIONS — Starting from the Main Street in Bunny, opposite the Rancliffe Arms, walk past the church to the end of the road. Turn right as footpath signed — East Leake 2¼ miles. The path is defined across the field and over Fairham Brook. Turn right by the brook and in 100 yards turn left at the path sign and walk up to the minor road. Cross over, as path signed, and follow a track which as you near the final slopes of the Bunny Hill bears slightly right and ascends to the wood. The path is defined in the wood and basically you go straight across bearing slightly left. Cross all tracks and reach a stile on the wood's other side. Bear half right across the fields, guided by the stiles, to reach a minor road in Bunny Hill, by stiles and path sign — East Leake. Cross the road to another stile and walk to the right of the houses on your left to the fields' far lefthand corner to a gate and path signs — Bunny/East Leake. Join a track and follow it to your right for 30 yards and turn left to walk around the field boundary to a stile. You now descend following an ill-defined path but there are stiles as you aim for the immediate right of Taft Leys Farm. There is a stile and footpath sign here.

Turn right and follow the hedged track for the next mile. First you ascend over the shoulder of the hill close to Trig point 95 metres on your right. On the other side you descend the zig-zag track to the minor road almost opposite Welldale Farm. Turn right along the road for 200 yards to a stile and footpath sign on your left. Go diagonally across the field to your right to a footbridge. Basically keep the same direction of travel with the field boundary on your left to reach the Fairham Brook in less than ½ mile and footbridge across it. Don't cross but turn right and walk beside the deep brook on your left, and in little over ½ mile you are back on your starting out path. Retrace your steps across the brook to the Main Street in Bunny.

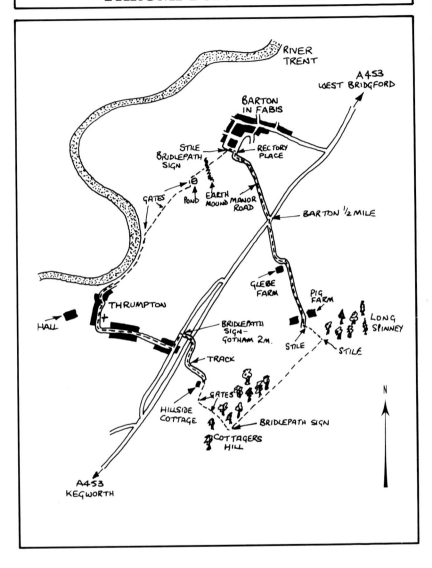

THRUMPTON AND GOTHAM HILL — 5 MILES

- allow 2¼ hours.

MAPS — O.S. 1:25,000 Pathfinder Series Sheet No 43/53 — Nottingham (South West).
- O.S. 1:50,000 Landranger Series Sheet No 129 — Nottingham & Loughborough area.

CAR PARK — No official one.

INN — None on the walk.

BASIC ROUTE — Thrumpton — Cottagers Hill — Gotham Hill — Glebe Farm — Barton in Fabis — River Trent — Thrumpton.

ABOUT THE WALK — A really magnificent walk that has everything you could ever want — attractive villages, wooded hills, distant views, and River Trent. During the summer you can include a visit to Thrumpton Hall.

WALKING INSTRUCTIONS — Starting from the church in Thrumpton, walk along the village road eastwards towards the A453 road. At the minor T junction turn left and 50 yards later turn right — signposted Public Bridleway — Gotham 2 miles. Cross the bridge over the A453 and follow the track round to your right. In 50 yards follow it to your left to soon pass a house on your right. Follow the track around the left of the house to a gate. Through this you soon bear left and ascend to a gate on the wood's edge. Continue straight ahead through the wood on the track to the other side where turn left, as bridlepath signed. Walk beside the wood on your left on a defined track. After ½ mile leave the wood behind as you keep to the crest of Gotham Hill. On nearing the start of another plantation ascend a stile at the footpath sign on your left. Cross the field and soon begin descending quite steeply to a stile on the left of the farm buildings below. The views to the Trent and beyond are exceptional here. Gaining the farm road turn right along it and along past Glebe Farm to the A453 road.

Cross over onto Manor Road signed — Barton ½ mile. Walk along the road for less than ½ mile to the start of the houses. Follow the road round to your right, and turn left into Rectory Place. A short distance along here turn left at the stile and bridleway sign. Most of the way to the River Trent ¾ mile away is on a track and it is well gated. First you cross an earth rampart then around a small pond before heading direct to the river. Follow the track beside the river on your right to Thrumpton. Reaching the road follow it round through the village back to the church.

THRUMPTON — The church dates from the 13th century and has several impressive monuments. It was restored in 1872. In the village you pass the impressive gateway to the Hall. The Hall was built by the Pigot family in the 17th century. The Charles 11 oak staircase is its most famous feature.

THRUMPTON CHURCH

THRUMPTON HALL GATEHOUSE

WHITE HOUSE INN, RIVER SOAR

ROSE AND CROWN INN, RIVER SOAR, ZOUCH

SUTTON BONINGTON — 5 MILES

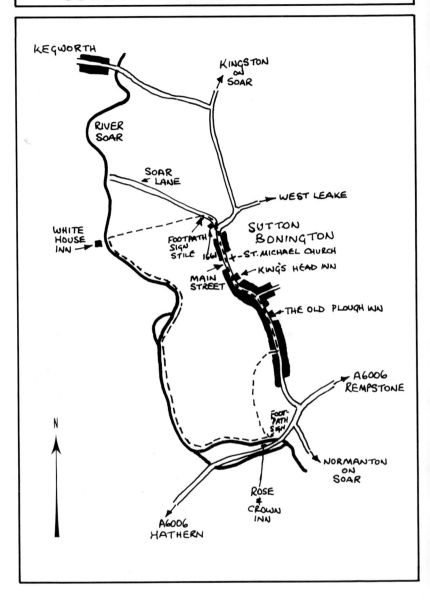

KEGWORTH

KINGSTON ON SOAR

RIVER SOAR

SOAR LANE

WEST LEAKE

WHITE HOUSE INN

SUTTON BONINGTON

FOOTPATH SIGN STILE 1661

ST. MICHAEL CHURCH

KING'S HEAD INN

MAIN STREET

THE OLD PLOUGH INN

A6006 REMPSTONE

N

FOOTPATH SIGN

NORMANTON ON SOAR

ROSE & CROWN INN

A6006 HATHERN

SUTTON BONINGTON AND RIVER SOAR —
5 MILES

- allow 2 hours.

MAPS — O.S. 1:25,000 Pathfinder Series Sheet No. SK 42/52
O.S. 1:50,000 Landranger Series Sheet No. 129 — Nottingham & Loughborough area.

CAR PARK — No official one.

INNS — King's Head, The Old Plough, Sutton Bonington; Rose and Crown,
Zouch.

BASIC ROUTE — Sutton Bonington — River Soar — Zouch — Sutton
Bonington.

ABOUT THE WALK — The River Soar forms part of the western boundary of
Nottinghamshire. From Sutton Bonington you cross the fields to the River Soar,
which is navigable, and leads to the Grand Union Canal, Loughborough and
Leicester. You walk beside the river for 2½ miles to Zouch and a riverside inn. A
path across the fields returns you to Sutton Bonington and the walk through the
village is very interesting with several old houses.

WALKING INSTRUCTIONS — Starting from the church, dedicated to St.
Michael, walk northwards along the Main Street out of the village. In 200 yards the
road turns sharp right. Keep straight ahead on Solar Lane, passing a gabled house
on your left dated 1661. Having left the houses behind turn left at the stile and
footpath sign on your left — you can continue ahead on the track to the river. Go
straight across the fields, which are well stiled, and reach the river in a little over ½
mile, opposite the White House Inn. Turn left and walk beside the river for the
next 2½ miles to Zouch and the Rose and Crown Inn opposite.

Just before gaining the road at Zouch turn left at the stile, footpath sign and
footbridge. Keep the field edge on your left and reach a gate and footbridge.
Continue ahead to a stile before bearing right towards the southern end of Sutton
Bonington. At the road turn left and follow the main road back to the church a mile
away.

SUTTON BONINGTON — was originally two — Sutton and Bonington — but
they have linked together and amalgamated their names. St. Michael's Church
dates from the 13th century and the 135 foot high spire is 14th Century.

THE RIVER SOAR — Several attempts were made to make the Soar navigable
but it wasn't until 1776 that the "Loughborough Canal" was begun and completed
two years later. The section from Loughborough to Leicester was completed in
1794. The canal was very prosperous because of its location to Nottingham and the
Erewash Canal. In 1931 the Grand Union Canal bought all the sections, making it
the Leicester Line — 66 miles long. The Sutton area is prone to flooding and the
fields you cross at the start of the walk are known as the flood plain.

WEST LEAKE HILLS — 4 MILES

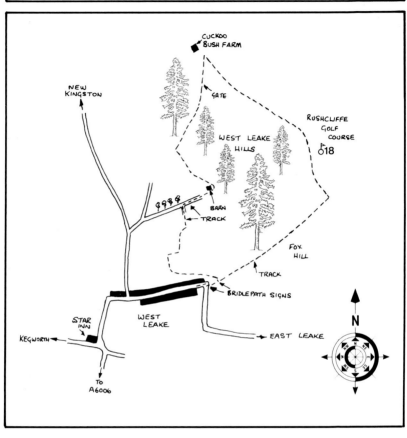

WEST LEAKE HILLS

WEST LEAKE HILLS — 4 MILES

- allow 1½ hours.

MAPS — O.S. 1:25,000 Pathfinder Series Sheet No SK42/52.
- O.S. 1:50,000 Landranger Series Sheet No 129 — Nottingham & Lough-borough area.

CAR PARK — No official one.

INN — None on the walk. Nearest just south of West Leake — The Star Inn.

BASIC ROUTE — West Leake — Fox Hill — Crow Wood Hill — Cuckoo Bush Farm — West Leake Hills — West Leake.

ABOUT THE WALK — Stunning! One of the most enjoyable and satisfying walks in Nottinghamshire. The whole walk is on well defined bridleways over hills, through woodland and across fields, with extensive views north to Nottingham and south to Loughborough. I cannot recommend this walk too highly.

WALKING INSTRUCTIONS — Start from the eastern side of West Leake, where the road turns sharp right by the last house. Here on the corner is the bridlepath sign. Walk through the gate opening and bear left and ascend the track up Fox Hill. Almost immediately on your left is another bridlepath sign and footbridge; this is your return route. Ascend the track over Fox Hill and in ¾ mile the track levels off and simply keep straight ahead for a further ½ mile to the righthand bend close to the edge of the hill. Turn left along the hill's edge with distant views and the Rushcliffe Golf Course on the right. Walk along the edge of the golf course for ½ mile before walking beside woodland on your left, then through a small woodland spur. Here you leave the golf course behind and continue beside the wood for a short while before it turns left. Keep ahead with the field boundary on your left as you walk towards Cuckoo Bush Farm and another wood.

On the edge of the wood go through the gate on your left and keep the field hedge on your right as you cross the field to the woodland of West Leake Hills, entered by a gate. Turn right on the track and this soon bears left and crosses the forest before descending a wide break to its southern end. Turn left along the wood's perimeter and reach a barn. Turn right onto a farm track and walk along this for ¼ mile to a row of trees. Just before them turn left on a track. This soon becomes a well defined path as you walk around the field edges back to the eastern side of West Leake where you began.

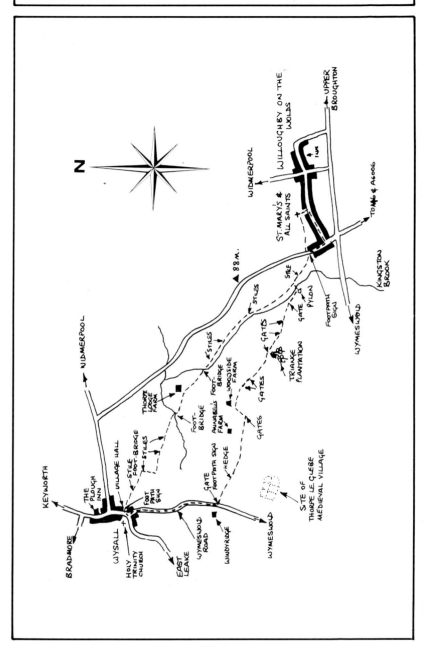

WILLOUGHBY-ON-THE-WOLDS — 6 MILES

- allow 2½ hours.

MAP — O.S. 1:25,000 Pathfinder Series Sheet No. SK 62/72 — Scalford and Nether Broughton.

CAR PARK — No official one.

INNS — None actually on the walk but just off it at Wysall is The Plough. Another is in Willoughby village on its eastern side.

BASIC ROUTE — Willoughby-on-the-Wolds — Kingston Brook — Triangle Plantation — Woodside Farm — Windyridge — Wystall — Thorpe Lodge Farm — Kingston Brook — Willoughby-on-the-Wolds.

ABOUT THE WALK — Originally I planned the walk to cross the site of the medieval villge of Thorpe le Glebe but the rights of way across it are hard to find and I had to reroute my plan and walk near it instead. There is not much to see on the ground — just mounds in a field. The walk despite this omission is attractive across the Nottinghamshire "wolds" close to the Leicestershire border. The two villages, linked together via paths and tracks across streams and by woods, are interesting with attractive churches rich in history.

WALKING INSTRUCTIONS — Starting from Willoughby you can follow the path from the church, dedicated to St. Mary and All Saints, across the fields to Wystall Road; it is well signed and stiled. Or you can walk along the Main Street to the road junction and turn right. In 200 yards almost opposite the last house is the footpath sign and stile; the church path reaches the road just ahead and you will have to turn left to reach this stile on your right. Cross the stile and descend the field to its bottom lefthand corner to a stile and footbridge. On your immediate left is Kingston Brook. Continue ahead to a footbridge over the brook close to an electric pylon on your left. Upon your return you will reach here and retrace your steps back to Willoughby.

Cross the footbridge and a few yards later bear right with the brook on your right to reach a gate. Through this leave the river and ascend to the gate in the top righthand corner. Keep the field boundary on your right to reach another gate and walk beside Triangle Plantation on your left, through gates to its end and a stile and footbridge. Cross this and turn right keeping the field boundary on your right. Close to the next wood go through a gate and bear left keeping the field boundary and wood on your immediate left to another gate. Continue ahead in the next field aiming for the lefthand side of Woodside Farm. Turn left near the field boundary and follow the track away from the farm to a gate by woodland. Turn right through this and follow the track, keeping straight ahead at all junctions and in just over ½ mile gain the minor road (Wysall/Wymeswold) via a gate opposite Windyridge. Turn right and follow the road for ½ mile to the main road in the village of Wysall.

Turn right along Main Street but almost immediately by the Village Hall, turn right as footpath signed. Past the houses you walk along the edge of a playing field and cross a footbridge. The next field has two stiles and in the next you walk around the field boundary to your right. The actuall path is well signed with yellow arrows and is well stiled. You walk beside two more fields to a footbridge over a stream. You then walk around the field edges to a stile near Thorpe Lodge Farm. You descend to your right to a stile and onto another and a footbridge over Kingston Brook. For the next mile to your starting out path you keep the brook on your right. The path is extremely well stiled and after about ten of them you are back opposite the pylon. Retrace your steps first by the brook and then up the field back to Willoughby village.

WILLOUGHBY-ON-THE-WOLDS — The church dates from the 12th Century and has monuments to the Willoughby family who remained associated with the village for 700 years. They built the Elizabethan Wollaton Hall in Nottingham which passed to the city in 1924. The Willoughbys gave their name to the village.

WYSALL — The church has Saxon masonry and a few Norman features, but most of it dates from the 13th-15th centuries. The spire is 650 years old.

WYSTALL CHURCH

VIEW FROM GOTHAM HILL

HOUSE DATED 1661, SOLAR LANE, SUTTON BONNINGTON

RUINED ST. MARY'S CHURCH, COLSTON BASSETT

SHELFORD LOCK

THE REINDEER INN, EAST BRIDGFORD

BOATS AT HAZELFORD FERRY

REMEMBER AND OBSERVE THE COUNTRY CODE

* Enjoy the countryside and respect its life and work.

* Guard against all risk of fire.

* Fasten all gates.

* Keep your dogs under close control.

* Keep to public paths across farmland.

* Use gates and stiles to cross fences, hedges and walls.

* Leave livestock, crops and machinery alone.

* Take your litter home — pack it in, pack it out.

* Help to keep all water clean.

* Protect wildlife, plants and trees.

* Take special care on country roads.

* Make no unnecessary noise.

RIVER TRENT AT GUNTHORPE FROM TRENT HILLS

THE HIKER'S CODE

* Hike only along marked routes — do not leave the trail.

* Use stiles to climb fences; close gates.

* Camp only in designated campsites.

* Carry a light-weight stove.

* Leave the Trail cleaner than you found it.

* Leave flowers and plants for others to enjoy.

* Keep dogs on a leash.

* Protect and do not disturb wildlife.

* Use the trail at your own risk.

* Leave only your thanks — take nothing but photographs.

STAR AND GARTER HOTEL, HAZELFORD FERRY

EQUIPMENT NOTES — some personal thoughts

<u>BOOTS</u> — preferably with a full leather upper, of medium weight, with a vibram sole. I always add a foam cushioned insole to help cushion the base of my feet.

<u>SOCKS</u> — I generally wear two thick pairs as this helps minimise blisters. The inner pair are of loop stitch variety and approximately 80% wool. The outer are a thick rib pair of approximately 80% wool.

<u>WATERPROOFS</u> — for general walking I wear a T shirt or shirt with a cotton wind jacket on top. You generate heat as you walk and I prefer to layer my clothes to avoid getting too hot. Depending on the season will dictate how many layers you wear. In soft rain I just use my wind jacket for I know it quickly dries out. In heavy downpours I slip on a neoprene lined cagoule, and although hot and clammy it does keep me reasonably dry. Only in extreme conditions will I don overtrousers, much preferring to get wet and feel comfortable.

<u>FOOD</u> — as I walk I carry bars of chocolate, for they provide instant energy and are light to carry. In winter a flask of hot coffee is welcome. I never carry water and find no hardship from not doing so, but this is a personal matter! From experience I find the more I drink the more I want and sweat. You should always carry some extra food such as Kendal mint cake, for emergencies.

<u>RUCKSACKS</u> — for day walking I use a climbing rucksac of about 40 litre capacity and although it leaves excess space it does mean that the sac is well padded, with an internal frame and padded shoulder straps. Inside apart from the basics for the day I carry gloves, balaclava, spare pullover and a pair of socks.

<u>MAP & COMPASS</u> — when I am walking I always have the relevant map — preferably the 1:25,000 scale — open in my hand. This enables me to constantly check that I am walking the right way. In case of bad weather I carry a compass, which once mastered gives you complete confidence in thick cloud or mist.

GRANTHAM CANAL NR KINOULTON

WALK RECORD CHART

Date Walked.

NEWARK ON TRENT — 6½ MILES ....*10 04 94*.........

FISKERTON — NORTH — 4½ MILES ....

FISKERTON — SOUTH — 4½ MILES ....

HOVERINGHAM — 5½ MILES ....*ALREADY WALKED*....

EAST BRIDGFORD — 5 MILES ....*1994*.........

LOWDHAM — 8 MILES ....

GUNTHORPE & BURTON JOYCE — 5 MILES ....

GUNTHORPE & CAYTHROPE — 4½ MILES ....

STOKE BARDOLPH — 5 MILES ....

FISKERTON TO COLWICH — 15 MILES ....

WHATTON — 5½ MILES ....

COLSTON BASSETT — 7 MILES ....

CLIPSTON — 4 MILES ....*16 04 94*.........

BUNNY — 6 MILES ....*26 2 94*.........

THRUMPTON — 5 MILES ....*ALREADY WALKED*....

SUTTON BONINGTON — 5 MILES ....*12 09 93*....

WEST LEAKE HILLS — 4 MILES ....*5 3 94*.........

WILLOUGHBY ON THE WOLDS — 6 MILES ....

HOVERINGHAM PASTURES SIGN

57

THE JOHN MERRILL WALK BADGE

THE JOHN MERRILL WALK BADGE — is available only to people who have walked six or more routes in this book. Send details or photocopy Walk Record Chart to JNM Publications.

Badges are circular; black cloth with figure embroidered in four colours and measure — 3½" in diameter.

BADGE ORDER FORM

Walks — Date completed ....

....

NAME ....

ADDRESS ....

....

Price: £2.00 each including postage, VAT and signed completion certificate.

From: **J.N.M. Publications, Winster, Matlock, Derbyshire, DE4 2DQ**
Tel: Winster (062988) 454 — 24hr answering service.
FAX: Winster (062988) 416

********* You may photocopy this form if needed ********

OTHER BOOKS BY JOHN N. MERRILL PUBLISHED BY JNM PUBLICATIONS

DAY WALK GUIDES -

SHORT CIRCULAR WALKS IN THE PEAK DISTRICT
LONG CIRCULAR WALKS IN THE PEAK DISTRICT
CIRCULAR WALKS IN WESTERN PEAKLAND
SHORT CIRCULAR WALKS IN THE STAFFORDSHIRE MOORLANDS
SHORT CIRCULAR WALKS AROUND THE TOWNS AND VILLAGES OF THE PEAK DISTRICT
SHORT CIRCULAR WALKS AROUND MATLOCK
SHORT CIRCULAR WALKS IN THE DUKERIES
SHORT CIRCULAR WALKS IN SOUTH YORKSHIRE
SHORT CIRCULAR WALKS AROUND DERBY
SHORT CIRCULAR WALKS AROUND BAKEWELL
SHORT CIRCULAR WALKS AROUND BUXTON
SHORT CIRCULAR WALKS IN SOUTH NOTTINGHAMSHIRE
SHORT CIRCULAR WALKS ON THE NORTHERN MOORS
40 SHORT CIRCULAR PEAK DISTRICT WALKS
SHORT CIRCULAR WALKS IN THE HOPE VALLEY

INSTRUCTION & RECORD -

HIKE TO BE FIT .... STROLLING WITH JOHN
THE JOHN MERRILL WALK RECORD BOOK

CANAL WALK GUIDES -

VOL ONE — DERBYSHIRE AND NOTTINGHAMSHIRE
VOL TWO — CHESHIRE AND STAFFORDSHIRE
VOL THREE — STAFFORDSHIRE
VOL FOUR — THE CHESHIRE RING
VOL FIVE — LINCOLNSHIRE & NOTTINGHAMSHIRE
VOL SIX — SOUTH YORKSHIRE
VOL SEVEN — THE TRENT & MERSEY CANAL

DAY CHALLENGE WALKS -

JOHN MERRILL'S WHITE PEAK CHALLENGE WALK
JOHN MERRILL'S YORKSHIRE DALES CHALLENGE WALK
JOHN MERRILL'S NORTH YORKSHIRE MOORS CHALLENGE WALK
PEAK DISTRICT END TO END WALKS
THE LITTLE JOHN CHALLENGE WALK
JOHN MERRILL'S LAKELAND CHALLENGE WALK
JOHN MERRILL'S STAFFORDSHIRE MOORLAND CHALLENGE WALK
JOHN MERRILL'S DARK PEAK CHALLENGE WALK

MULTIPLE DAY WALKS -

THE RIVERS' WAY
PEAK DISTRICT HIGH LEVEL ROUTE
PEAK DISTRICT MARATHONS
THE LIMEY WAY
THE PEAKLAND WAY

COAST WALKS -

ISLE OF WIGHT COAST WALK
PEMBROKESHIRE COAST PATH
THE CLEVELAND WAY

HISTORICAL GUIDES -

DERBYSHIRE INNS — an A to Z Guide
HALLS AND CASTLES OF THE PEAK DISTRICT & DERBYSHIRE
TOURING THE PEAK DISTRICT AND DERBYSHIRE BY CAR
DERBYSHIRE FOLKLORE
LOST INDUSTRIES OF DERBYSHIRE
PUNISHMENT IN DERBYSHIRE
CUSTOMS OF THE PEAK DISTRICT AND DERBYSHIRE
WINSTER — a SOUVENIR GUIDE
ARKWRIGHT OF CROMFORD
TALES FROM THE MINES by GEOFFREY CARR
PEAK DISTRICT PLACE NAMES by MARTIN SPRAY

JOHN'S MARATHON WALKS -

TURN RIGHT AT LAND'S END
WITH MUSTARD ON MY BACK
TURN RIGHT AT DEATH VALLEY
EMERALD COAST WALK

COLOUR GUIDES -

THE PEAK DISTRICT...................................Something to remember her by.

SKETCH BOOKS — by John Creber

NORTH STAFFORDSHIRE SKETCHBOOK

CALENDARS

1989 JOHN MERRILL PEAK DISTRICT WALK A MONTH CALENDAR